Contents

1 The Concert

The concert hall in the palace was full.
Everyone was excited.
The Royal concerts were always wonderful.
But this one was going to be different.

There was a hush as a young musician
went up on the stage.
He bowed to the Royal Family
and sat down at the piano.
He raised his hands and began to play.

The music filled the hall.
It was beautiful music.
It held the audience in a spell.
The musician's skill was amazing.

When he finished playing,
everyone stood up.
They clapped and cheered.
The musician bowed to the Royal Family
and left the stage.

'That was wonderful!' said the Emperor.
'I must meet him.'

So the Emperor was taken to meet the player.
'Tell me, how old are you?' asked the Emperor.

'I am five years old,' said the young boy, smiling.

The boy's father touched him gently on the shoulder.
He was so proud of his son,
Wolfgang Amadeus Mozart.

Mozart plays for the Royal Family.

2 Childhood

Wolfgang Mozart was born on 27 January 1756
in Salzburg, Austria.
His mother, Anna, gave birth to seven children.
But only two of them lived.
The oldest child, a girl named Nannerl,
and the youngest, Wolfgang.

Mozart was a small, thin child.
As an infant he was very ill
and nearly died.
But he was a happy child
and he loved playing tricks and jokes
on his sister Nannerl.

Leopold, Mozart's father,
was a musician.
He played the violin, the organ
and the clavier (an early piano).
Nannerl was musical too.
She could play the clavier when she was five.

Mozart's talent was spotted by his father
when he was very young.
By the age of four,
he only had to listen to his father sing a tune
and he could play it on the clavier, note for note.

By the age of six,
Mozart was writing his own music.
He wrote music for a dance called a minuet.
He ran to show it to his father.
The ink was smudged all over the page
and at first, Leopold thought it was a joke.
But then he looked closer
and saw that every note was perfect.
His six year old son had written
a beautiful piece of music.

Leopold loved his children
but he was a strict father.
He had great plans for his talented children.
He felt he had failed as a musician
and wanted his children to succeed.

When Mozart was six and his sister was eleven,
he took them on a tour.
They were going to play
at all the Royal Courts in Europe.

3 Touring

The children and their father
made the long journeys by mail coach.
The mail coach was cramped, cold and slow.
It went at about 8 miles per hour
over bumpy roads.

The family arrived in Munich in 1762.
Rich people invited them into their homes to play.

People soon got to hear
about the talented children.
Mozart would perform musical tricks
on the piano.
He would play a difficult piece
with only one finger.
And he would play with a cloth
covering the keyboard,
so he couldn't see the keys.
Not a note was out of place.

In Vienna, Mozart became very ill
with scarlet fever.
Again, he nearly died.
The family returned home.
But Leopold was already planning the next tour.

The next tour lasted three and a half years.
Mozart and his sister
played before all the courts of Europe.
They played before the King and Queen of France
and the King and Queen of England.

In London, Mozart met the famous musician,
J C Bach.
Bach was 30 and Mozart was only eight.
But they became good friends
and often played music together.
They never met again after this tour,
but they wrote letters to each other
for the next 28 years.

Some people thought Mozart must be older
because he played so well.
A musical expert decided to test him.
He gave him music to play
and asked him to compose pieces.
Mozart played and composed like an adult.
But between the tests he played games.
He ran around the room on a broom,
pretending it was a horse.
There was no doubt –
this amazing child really was only eight years old.

On the way back,
Nannerl became very ill with typhoid
and *she* almost died.
Then Mozart caught it.
'He looked like nothing more than skin and bone,'
said his father.
The tour had been hard on the children.
But Leopold had made money from it.
And Mozart was now famous all over Europe.

4 His First Opera

When he was ten,
Mozart was asked to write an opera
for the Court in Vienna.
An opera is a play set to music.

Mozart was thrilled.
But the other musicians at the Court were jealous
of this ten year old boy.
They refused to work with him.
The opera was never performed.

When Mozart was 13,
his father took him on a tour of Italy.
Italy was the home of opera.
They arrived at Milan in the carnival season.
Mozart loved the parties and concerts.

And people loved it when Mozart played.
He was a great success in Italy.
Everyone had heard of him.
People waved at him in the streets.

He was asked to write another opera.
This time, it was performed.
People loved it.
The theatre where it was playing
was full every night.

Mozart's father, Leopold, had a job as a musician
at the Court of Salzburg.
He got on well with his employer, the Archduke,
who allowed him to travel with Mozart.
Leopold wanted Mozart to get a job
with the Court orchestra too.

Sadly, the Archduke died
the day after they got home to Salzburg,
and the new Archduke was not so friendly.

Conducting the Court Orchestra.
This photo is from a film about Mozart's life.

5 Trouble At Work

The new Archduke, Colleredo,
did not like Mozart or his father.
He didn't let them go off touring.
He wanted them to stay at Court,
to do as they were told.
He thought musicians were servants.
He was also a very tall man
and he didn't like short people.
Mozart was only five feet tall,
so they were never going to be the best of friends.

Mozart thought Colleredo was a fool.
Colleredo knew nothing about music.
But Mozart needed a job.
When he was 16,
Colleredo offered him a job.
It was as leader of the Court Orchestra.
Mozart had to take it.

It was not well paid.
But it gave Mozart the chance to write music.
Sometimes, Colleredo would let him go
on a short tour.
But he wasn't paid while he was away
and he always felt trapped when he got back.
He found it hard to hide his dislike of Colleredo.
After two unhappy years, Mozart was asked to leave.

He went to Paris with his mother
and earned a little money
by playing and teaching music.
But it was not enough.
Every night, he went out drinking,
meeting people and making friends.
Soon he had money troubles.
This was the story of Mozart's life –
he was good at spending money
but bad at earning it.

Then Mozart's mother became ill.
She died in July 1778.
Mozart was heartbroken.

There was nothing Mozart could do
but go back and work for Colleredo again.
He felt even more trapped than before.
He didn't get on so well with his father now.
His father didn't like him going out to parties
and drinking every night.
In 1780, Colleredo allowed Mozart
to go to the carnival in Munich.
Mozart had been asked to write an opera for it.

'But you'd better be back on time,'
said Colleredo. 'Or there'll be trouble.'

Mozart had a wonderful time at the carnival.
And, of course,
he was weeks late getting back to work.

Colleredo was furious.
'I'm not letting you travel again!' he said.
'Remember that you are a servant.
You must eat with the servants.
And you must be ready to perform for me
whenever I say so.'

This was too much.
Mozart left the job.

Now he had no job and no money.
But at least he was free.

6 Marriage

Mozart went to Vienna.
He earned a little money by teaching.
Every day, he wrote music.

Every night, he went out to parties.
He loved meeting people
and having a good time.

One of his friends said of him:
'Mozart loved dancing.
He was a very small man.
He was thin and pale with fine, fair hair.'

Mozart could speak four languages –
German, French, Italian and English.
He could play every instrument there was.
He had perfect pitch –
he could name a note just by hearing it.

While in Vienna, Mozart fell in love
with Constanze Weber.
He knew the Weber family well.
A few years earlier, he had fallen in love
with Constanze's older sister.
Mozart's father had said they couldn't get married.
This time, Mozart was not going to be put off.
He asked Constanze to marry him in December 1781.
The wedding took place in August 1782.

The day after the wedding a letter arrived.
It was from Leopold, Mozart's father.
He gave the marriage his blessing.

7 Family Life – And Death

Mozart and Constanze were very happy together.
They understood each other.
They both loved going out and having fun.
The only trouble was,
they never had enough money.

Soon, there was a baby on the way.
It was a baby boy.
Mozart loved the child.

But Leopold had still not met Constanze.
So Mozart and Constanze went to Salzburg
to see him.
They did not take the baby.
They thought the long journey
might be dangerous for him,
so they left the baby with foster parents.

When they got back,
the baby had died.
Illness and disease took many young lives
in those days.
Constanze gave birth to seven children
but only two lived.
This was just like Mozart's own mother.

Mozart was heartbroken
every time one of his children died.
He could only cope by working.
His sadness poured out of him through his music.
He turned his sorrow into something beautiful.
A writer on Mozart has said:
'Happiness and sorrow play
like sunlight and shadow
through Mozart's music.'

He had to give music lessons to earn money.
Sometimes he didn't have time
to prepare for his concerts.
He would have to write the music
on the night of the concert.
But he could do this,
because writing music came so easily to him.
He could hear the music in his head,
then write it down without needing to change a note.
It would always be perfect.

8 Figaro

In 1785, the Emperor asked Mozart
to write a comic opera.
Mozart worked with a partner, Lorenzo,
who wrote the words to Mozart's music.
The opera was first performed on 1 May 1786.
It was called *The Marriage of Figaro*,
and was a great success.

Mozart wrote,
'Here they talk about nothing but *Figaro*.
Nothing is played, sung or whistled but *Figaro*.'

It was such a success that
Mozart and Lorenzo worked together again.
The next opera was called *Don Giovanni*.
The night before the first performance,
Mozart hadn't finished the music!

Constanze thought he would have finished it
and had planned a big party.
Mozart went to the party.
He drank a lot of wine and danced.
But Constanze pulled him away
because she knew he had to finish the opera.

ENO

Mozart

Figaro's Wedding

February 14 17 20 28
March 4 6 8 11 13
18 20 at 7.00pm
March 15 at 6.30pm

Figaro is still popular today.
Sometimes the opera is called *Figaro's Wedding*.

They sat together in a room
as the candles burned.
Constanze kept Mozart awake,
drinking with him and talking to him.
Mozart wrote down his music.
And the music was wonderful.

But the stress of living and working like this
began to show.
Both Mozart and Constanze became ill.
During this time, Leopold had died.
Mozart was heartbroken,
but too ill even to go to his father's funeral.

In November 1787,
Mozart was made Court Composer in Vienna.
He wrote music for the Emperor.
He thought of his father.
How proud he would have been.

The job was an honour –
but it was not well paid.
Mozart and Constanze
still spent more than they earned.

9 The Man In Black

By the time he was 35 years old,
Mozart had written over 700 pieces of music.
But he had earned little money from them.
He had to borrow from friends.
The stress of too much work
and not enough money made his illness worse.

Mozart was working on another opera,
The Magic Flute.
Constanze was expecting another baby.
Maybe their life would get better?

The day after their son was born,
there was a knock at the door.
Mozart was busy working.
He was tired and didn't feel well.
He didn't want any visitors,
but he opened the door.

A thin, pale man in black stood there.
Mozart couldn't see the man's face.
'I want you to write something for me,'
said the man.
He gave Mozart a letter,
then turned and walked away.

Mozart felt afraid.
There was something strange about the man.
In the letter, Mozart was asked to write
a Requiem Mass,
a solemn piece of music
to be played at a funeral.

Mozart finished *The Magic Flute*,
which was a success.
But the man in black was still on his mind.

One day Mozart was out with Constanze
and they saw the man again.
The man took hold of Constanze's arm.
'Tell me, how is the Requiem coming along?'
he asked.
'When will it be finished?'

Mozart could not get the man in black
out of his mind.

10 The Funeral

To Mozart, the man in black was a sign.
A sign of his own death.
He believed he was writing
a Requiem for his own funeral.

Mozart began to imagine he had been poisoned.
He had fainting fits
and terrible headaches.
The little energy he had left
went into the Requiem.
He had to get it finished.

He wrote to his friend, Lorenzo:
'My end has come
before I was able to profit from my talent.
And yet life has been so beautiful.
Nobody can change his Fate.'

It was 4 December 1791.
The candles flickered.
They were burning low.
Mozart was sitting up in bed.
He was too weak to write.
The music was in his head.
The final notes for his unfinished Requiem.

Constanze called for Mozart's student.
'He needs you,' she said.

The student sat close to Mozart.
Mozart spoke carefully.
He explained, note by note,
how the Requiem should end.
And the student wrote it down.

It was midnight.
Constanze sat with her husband.
He was slipping away from her.
How they had loved each other!
She was overcome with grief.

At one in the morning, Mozart died.
He was 35 years old.

It was a cheap funeral.
There was a light mist in Vienna.
A few friends followed
the funeral carriage to the church.

It was a short service.
The coffin was taken to the cemetery.
Snow began to fall.
Mozart's body was taken out of the coffin.
It was dumped in an unmarked grave
with five other bodies.
To this day, nobody knows where Mozart's grave is.

Wolfgang Amadeus Mozart.
This portrait was painted when he was 21.

Mozart's Life

January 1756	Mozart born in Salzburg.
1762	Writes first minuet at the age of six.
1763–1767	Tours Europe, performing with his sister Nannerl.
1768	Writes his first opera.
1772	He becomes leader of the Court Orchestra in Salzburg.
1778	His mother dies in Paris.
1781	He leaves Salzburg after falling out with Archduke Colleredo.
1782	He settles in Vienna and marries Constanze Weber.
1786	Writes *The Marriage of Figaro*.
1787	His father dies.
1791	Writes a Requiem for a mysterious man in black. Some experts today think it was Count Walsegg, who wanted the Requiem for his wife.
4 December 1791	Mozart dies aged 35.